The Hunt for Nok

Karen Ball • Jonatronix

OXFORD
UNIVERSITY PRESS

Max's mission log

We are travelling through space on board the micro-ship Excelsa with our new friends, Nok and Seven.

We're on a mission to save Planet Exis (Nok's home planet), which is running out of power. We need to collect four fragments that have been hidden throughout the Beta-Prime Galaxy. Together the fragments form the Core of Exis. Only the Core will restore power to the planet.

It's not easy. A space villain called Badlaw wants the power of the Core for himself. His army of robotic Krools is never far behind us!

Fragments collected so far: 1

In our last adventure ...

Cat, Nok and I were chased by some strange cats called pyrite panthers. They belonged to a Minatroll.

The Minatroll captured us in a ruby cage. Cat and I managed to shrink and escape, but Nok's shrinking button didn't work.

Another Minatroll turned up and they took Nok away on a cart.

Chapter 1 – Storm surprise

Max and Cat bent low over their holo-boards. They raced across the surface of Celeston in search of Nok. He had been captured by some Minatrolls.

Soon, they spotted the huge Minatrolls up ahead. Nok was trapped in a ruby cage. The pyrite panthers were pulling him on a cart.

"Hurry up, Max," Cat urged, speeding ahead.

Minatrolls

Information

Minatrolls are some of the most bad-tempered aliens in the galaxy. They wear armour made from tough, ruby-red crystals. They can shoot red mineral rays from the bands on their wrists.

Diet

Mineral mash, made from ground-up rocks.

Habitat

Minatrolls live in the crystal caves on Celeston.

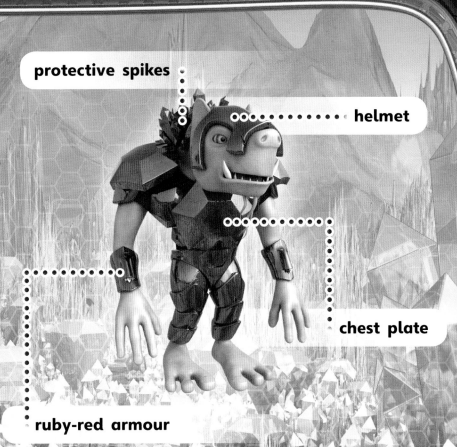

protective spikes

helmet

chest plate

ruby-red armour

Camouflage

The armour the Minatrolls wear can change colour. This means they can camouflage themselves against the crystal rocks on the planet.

"Wait!" said Max, staring at a huge cloud of dust in the distance. "It's a mineral storm. We need to hide."

They watched as the Minatrolls walked straight into the swirling dust.

"What about Nok?" Cat called back.

"We don't have a choice," replied Max. "We have to get out of the storm."

They landed their holo-boards and looked around for somewhere to shelter. Max spotted a small hole in a pile of rocks. They shrank and ran inside just as the storm hit.

They watched the storm sweep across the landscape. Mineral rain thundered down.

At last the clouds cleared and Max
and Cat were able to leave their shelter.

They grew back to normal size.

Just then, Cat heard a scuffling noise
not far off.

"What's that?" she whispered.

Chapter 2 – Panther rescue

Cat hurried over to a large crack in the ground. "Max!" she called.

Max peered down and saw a pyrite panther trapped below. It was scratching the walls.

"It must have become separated from the others in the storm," Max said. "We have to help it."

Max and Cat pressed the buttons on their spacesuits and their wings unfolded.

They flew down to the panther. Part of its harness was caught under a large rock.

The panther snarled at them.

"Easy," said Cat softly. "We're trying to help you." She stroked its head and soon it was calm.

Max gently unclipped the harness from the panther's collar.

"Now let's get you out of here," said Max.

Together Max and Cat lifted the panther and flew it back up to safety.

"It's really heavy!" Cat said.

"We're nearly there," Max replied. "Just keep going."

As soon as they reached the top, the panther leapt out of their arms. It ran in the direction the Minatrolls had gone.

"Come on!" Cat cried, flying after the panther. "It might lead us to Nok!"

The panther bounded along the rocky track. Max and Cat followed behind.

Soon, they came to a huge pyramid. It was shaped out of jagged shards of coloured stone.

"It's the pyramid we saw on the map in the cave!" exclaimed Cat.

"That means the fragment must be here, too," Max said.

The pyramid was surrounded by a moat of hot bubbling, red liquid. They could feel the heat rising off it. Their wings began to flicker and fade from the heat.

"We need to land!" said Max.

The panther stalked up to the edge of the moat. Then it stared up at the pyramid.

"It wants to get inside. Maybe that's where the Minatrolls have taken Nok," Cat said.

Max and Cat saw a path of stepping stones right across the moat.

"It looks like that's the only way across," said Cat.

The panther leapt on to the first stone. It jumped again, avoiding a smaller stone.

Max went first. He stepped on to the stone that the panther had missed. It started to sink into the moat.

"Follow the path the panther is taking!" Cat cried. "It must know which ones are safe."

Carefully they made their way across the moat.

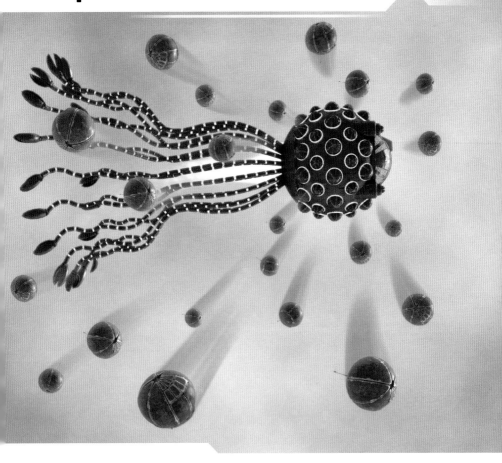

Max heard a loud rumble in the sky. Hovering overhead was a spaceship.

"Krools!" he cried.

Suddenly, metallic green balls started raining down. As they landed, Badlaw's deadly robots split open ready for action.

Max and Cat ran across the last of the
stepping stones. They pressed themselves
against the side of the pyramid. More
and more Krools landed at the edge of
the moat.

"There are so many of them!"
Cat gasped.

One of the Krools tried to cross the stepping stones. It took a wrong step and sank into the bubbling liquid.

"It won't be long before they make it across," Max said. "We need to get inside the pyramid, quickly."

The panther put its paw on a statue next to the entrance. The door slid open.

Max and Cat followed the panther inside, and the door slammed shut behind them. The pyrite panther ran off and they were all alone.

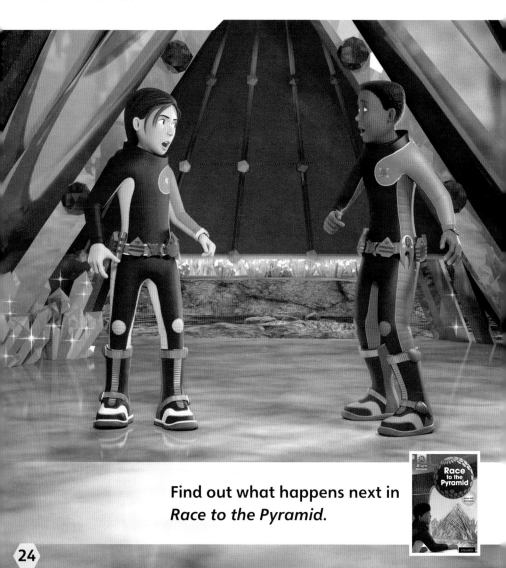

Find out what happens next in *Race to the Pyramid.*